JN440177

Cave Boys

Cave Boys

A collection of new poems by Lee Sul-ya
Translated by Brother Anthony of Taizé

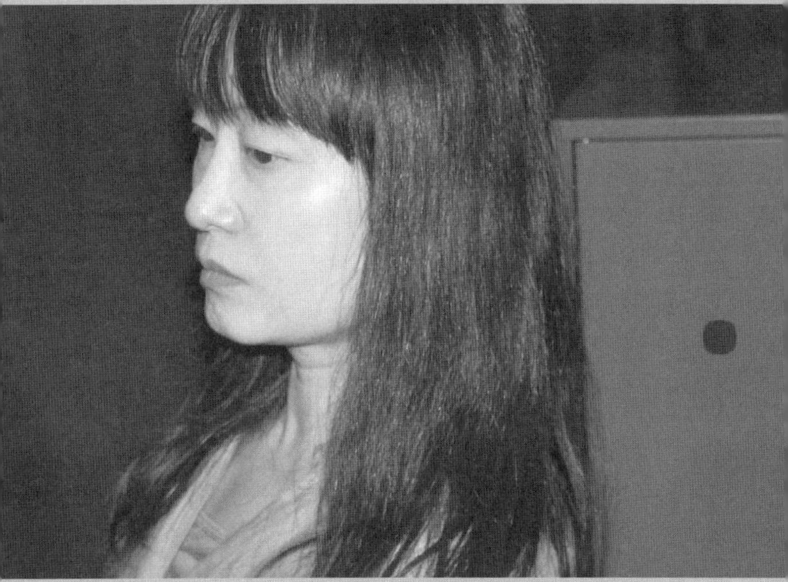

아시아

Contents

CAVE BOYS

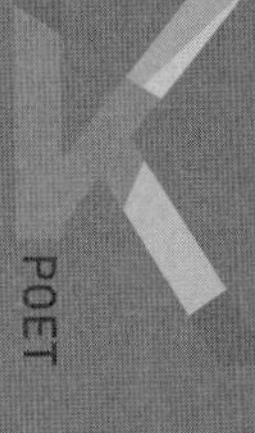

A Child who Lost a Parrot

Little child.

Let me take the bird out of you.

Let me take out the bird trapped in your mouth.

There was a family that kept Macau parrots.
Zohra Shah, the home help,
took care of the baby.

Four expensive parrots lived in a cage
then one of them went flying away by mistake.
The cage was only open for a moment to feed them
and in a flash one bird disappeared by mistake,

a world disappeared.

The little Pakistani girl Zohra Shah was only eight years old.

She changed the baby's diaper with her small hands and swept the yard.

She lost the Macau parrot

that she couldn't even look at for the rest of her life with her few pennies.

Where did the bird's footprints go flying off,

scattering like clouds?

She was beaten by the owner; her bones were

crushed.

The girl went flying into the sky that had swallowed the bird.

Sher spread her wings and went flying out of the great cage,

over the bridge of clouds.

In the little village where the girl once lived,

white feathers scattered like snow.

Had the bird disappeared into the pocket of an angel?

The child went flying to heaven looking for the bird.

But there are no birds in heaven.

There are only dead birds,

birds blinded, dying in search of God.

There are only birds that die as they go.

Little child.

Let me take you out of the bird.

Let me take you out, trapped as you are in the bird's beak.

Cave Boys

Darkness at midday,
acrid smoke rolling up to the edge of the sky,
darkness with darkness fell before history,
young boys forced onto the black trains and sent off somewhere,
not knowing where they are, whether they close their eyes or open their eyes,
deep in the mountain, a cave with red water flowing down.

The Japanese dug holes in the cave walls and installed dynamite.
The burrowing boys rushed outside.

An explosion rang out, clouds of smoke went billowing up
and once the stone dust reached the mouth of the cave,
the boys went back in
then came out again clasping rocks to their chests.

From dawn till late at night, the boys dug the cave
and when their nails fell out, the blood wouldn't stop.

It was too dark in the cave
so when rocks fell, they broke their limbs,

If only they could take the sun and the moon into the cave
would the heavy stones disappear?

They felt as if their bones were shattering at the sound of chisels struck each day
in the Bupyeong underground caves, where stalactites flow like tears.*

Other boys brought with them were assigned to the

* A total of 24 underground galleries (caves), dug out during the Pacific War by young Korean students forcibly mobilized by the Japanese, have been discovered so far.

arsenal.[**] and

Mitsubishi Steel[***]

They used to load up weapons and hide them in every cavern.

Dead boys wander like clouds.

We used to listen to what the people who discovered the cave said.

** The arsenal was a military arsenal built by the Japanese.

*** a Japanese company guilty of war crimes, it produced military supplies and supplied them to the arsenal.

Here, where footprints of red water pool,
rusty locks melt like red tears,
the deep, deep craters
the joints of old time trapped in the dark caves.

The boys kept on digging the caves, not even knowing they were dead when they died.
Keeping on digging,
digging into their hardened hearts,
boys who did not die, though they died,
still digging the caves though dead,

the cave boys.

Snowman

Looking at the smoke from the black factory chimney
in the drifting snow
I wait for you who will not come.
Along multiple roads in the blizzard
I came, a long while,
and the more I walked
the bigger the white mounds of snow grew.

As I look back,
the road is being erased.
As I look back again,
my footprints are frozen there.

Become like

snow perched on trees with broken branches,

rock-like snow,

snow turned into trees,

become like that.

Snow is falling,

falling and piling up.

Snow is falling,

telling me not to look ahead,

erasing my eyes.

Fully erased,

I become a huge snowman.

Snow
comes falling, telling me
not to see anything,
the dead eyes inside me,
eyes returning as blizzards.

A Butterfly's Torn Shoulders

I just tore the wings off a butterfly and ate them.

When I opened my eyes, there I was, lying on a wet mat, flowing on.

Let's turn back the clock.

I was looking out of the car window.

The rescue team had arrived

but the man didn't stand up.

Let's go a lot farther back in time.

From above the ceiling someone watched me fall from the stairs.

My shoulder shattered instead of my face.

The air broke into pieces.

The magnolia petals that fell today are getting rained on.
I took out a bunch of crying branches,
the magnolia's shivering shoulders.

The shoulder blades were barely attached
but I was there, unable to go back to what I was before.
I was smiling as if I was smiling,
unable to walk shoulder to shoulder with you anymore.

After only listening to the songs I want to hear,
only looking at the flowers I want to see,
I got rid of the butterfly's wings.
A butterfly that just disappeared in a few seconds.
There I was, holding on to my wings that couldn't turn back.

There I was, neatly collecting broken bones on the grass,
ironing folded wings,
enjoying the tilted position.

I closed my eyes and then opened them slowly.

Butterfly's wings starting to grow back from my armpits.

A morning when the secrets of life awake.

Kindness

My kindness in watering that tree every day is a pain that takes its breath away. Maybe it's heavy rain pouring down on a grove of young trees. Cats that come crushing the night's lights on a street with closed doors, the way the cats leaning on the outside wall of the collapsing building did not run away shows that I was accepted as a kindred species, or was seriously injured,

An evening when crickets raise their antennae to receive all kinds of sounds. My laughter is a current of pain piercing the cat's brain, or perhaps a sharp blade that rips through its heart.

Pussy, pussy

I'll give you food, give me a tender heart,

small and lovely cat.

The cat, avoiding my footsteps, disappeared in an instant into an underground cliff, missing its hand that barely reached through the crack in the wall. When I went down to the cellar, the cat was turning into a flat corner. My kindness drove the rain down to the basement and the cat was turning into something that wasn't a cat.

Last night the baby spiders died and left my house,

the leaves I touched screamed and fell as they left.

When I went back downstairs with a flashlight and a carrying bag, the cat was gone. The large underground warehouse is getting smaller and smaller like a cat, and I'm also getting as small as a cat, and at some point I fell into the rain-swept forest and chased after a gray cat.

Pussy, pussy,

I'll give you a flower. Give me a glass bead.

Come flying. Come and listen to my song.

The night cat, with a face that did not wear out though it wiped and wiped it, was hiding words in its claws. It was crushing the night's last gleams of light.

The short-circuited kindness was soaked in rain, the wings of the butterfly were getting wet, and I was turning into something that was no longer me.

Restavek*

"If I fall, the one and only tree of liberty
in Saint-Domingue will fall.
Yet the tree of liberty will rise again,
and will put forth many new roots deep in the earth."**

1.

Whips sell like hot cakes in the market.
Black girls and boys become Restaveks once they

* 'avec' (together) and 'rester' (stay) is a French compound word, and refers to a child in Haiti who lives in another house and does all the housework without being paid a penny. Mostly they are from 4 to 15 years old. It is illegal not to pay wages to people over 15 years old, so they are usually kicked out onto the streets at this age.

** To this day, every Haitian student can recite the last words of Louverture when he was being taken to France. (Noam Chomsky, Year 501: The Conquest Continues.)

are over four years old.

Restavek is the language of the occupants who threw their children into hell.

Born in the land where the first black slave revolution took place,

the children of poor families become slaves in other houses.

Even in their dreams, the whip comes snaking and they awake with blue bruises.

2.

It was a huge sugar factory.
Black slaves arriving at the sugar cane field
with their left hand tied to their left foot
their right hand tied to their right foot,
work muzzled with cans.
No matter how hungry they are, they can't eat a piece of sugarcane,
like cormorants that can't swallow a single fish
because of the thread wrapped around their necks.

With chains around their necks,
they work day and night until their nails fall off.

All the trees in the mountains and fields that used to be straight and dense have disappeared.

Betwitched,

the grandfathers of the grandfathers who only worked

became zombies.

Still chained, even as souls,

they come out of the grave and cut the sugar cane.

Even when they die, they can't get away from work.

3.

Kids eat mud cookies once a day or, if they're lucky, twice.

They won't eat real sweet cookies until they die.

There will be an earthquake soon.

They will become Restaveks and live with a frightening master.

Children who grew up on mud cookies wander around the world like ghosts when they grow up.

Even if they take advantage of the night to cross the border, they still can't own anything as if in their own land.

They survive the dark black nights.

Revolution is like a mirage

It's too far-fetched.

Although it was independent, it was robbed for one hundred and twenty-two years as compensation,

while the sky over the Eiffel Tower is high and blue.

Descendants of the rich Caribbean

they live and walk on the poorest land.

Selling children who grew up in slavery
back into slavery,
that's a skill learned from the gods of the white men.

4.

The island of Espanola, discovered by Columbus, is dazzlingly beautiful.

The songs of the waves spreading across the Caribbean hide their sorrow
and send clouds rising to the horizon.

Poor seeds were submerged.

5.

While black girls sew torn souls

the masters feast every night, drinking French wine.

While the voodoo dolls cry instead of the girls

even the hot sun hides in the waves for a while.

Black-faced girls become Restavecs even if they

are reborn.

They have to be given back their gods.

The dreams that still remain are crumbling like mud.

6.

Whips will sell like hot cakes in the markets tomorrow as well.

Nights when even the shadows of black girls and boys

who whispered the name of the god who created the sun
are torn apart by the whip

A living tree trembling next to a dead tree

Black roots wrapping around each other's necks

Tomorrow coming and going

Prison of Words

In your mouth that says you want to die
there is the fallen knee of the rock
and the fear of a roof on which thunder is rolling

When you keep saying like a frequent phone call
that you'll die, do you really mean that you want to die?
Saying: My stomach hurts so much I'll die,
saying: I hate you so much I'll die,
words that say you won't die even if you say you want to die

Trees weeping in the rain,

birds swallowing the words of dead trees in their mouths
won't die even if they die.
Therefore, saying: I love you so much that I'll die,
saying: I miss you so much that I'll die,
means you won't ever die.

Words filling the air uncertainly like black plastic bags,
how far do your old words
go after flowing down from plastered walls?

Words are dying

In the words “be careful”

the words “Don’t die” are dying hidden,

slowly dying.

Finally

horror attained,

another Hell.

Snowflakes Eager to Become Snowmen

I pack my daydreams every day. I open empty boxes and bags, stack up canned food neatly, only increasing books with torn leaves, I don't go home. I don't go to school anymore, either.

Until the sun that once rattled the window and laughed vanishes behind the evening star, until it pushes my back, until the earth bends its back I sometimes lose my home at home. The sun and the stars, setting fire to the house that was once a tree, move about with the sea, the home of waves, attached to their toes.

I'm always the person who leaves, the person who has to leave, the person who walks and walks until the clouds turn to snow, the person who becomes a snowflake and wants to fall anywhere, I go on to meet you who are nowhere, not the next stop, not the next stop.

Wiping a mirror covered in thin ice, I live the season of glaciers. Then the snow that clinks like ice with falling snow with someone falling, fluttering snowflakes, become a snowman as I go wandering through the night of footprints on snow chasing white shadows.

Saint-Nazaire in my Dreams

When you went to Saint-Nazaire, the first thing you did was write me a letter. But the letter only reached me after you and I had parted. As soon as I got the letter, I sent it back to you. Your room had no light at all. Light creates shadows, but shadows only increase shadows. Leaves also increased the shadows. A room where the moonlight used to melt.

It was a day when many Sundays had been spent, and the April fish sparkled. When I went to Saint-Nazaire in search of you, you were nowhere to be found, as if you were not on the earth. I couldn't understand the people there at all. I erased your days while collecting life in a foreign country. I dreamed that I was an I who was no longer me

Every dream was full of relics. In the morning I would grab the ankles of the mist that puts the bronze mirror in the coffin. You discovered me, who had become you, among the relics. Okla.

Okla. Take a look at the records of the refugees!

When morning comes soon, everyone will leave from here,

I'll run out of my dreams

Okla. I don't even know who you are.

Get out of my dream right now!

These mists,

Okla, wait!

Before you leave my dreams, get me out of my dreams!

Hurry up and break that hazy glass window!

I have finally left your dreams

and now I stand outside your dreams.

Ant Hell

The boys
who used to play hide and seek around the drains at the construction site
gather in corners of sandy mountains to create an ant hell.

After digging a deep hole, they spread newspaper like a trap,
covering it with grains of sand
so that the road continued intact,
they made a road that was not a road

One ant carrying honey, maybe friend, maybe foe,

disappeared into a grain of sand.

The ground where shadows knowing nothing of tomorrow gather,

if it rains, the ant hell will disappear.

The unknowable Hell

and the equally unknowable Heaven.

Hey, the ant-faced kid

is coming, hide.

Wind, a child

fell out.

The ant Hell where the more you try to get out, the

more you get sucked in,

In Hell, Hell is unknown,
Only Hell is repeated

Covered in black newspapers
even dirtier boys
came running out of the sand.

Wind,
quick, hide.
To the ant hell where ant ghosts are waiting,
swallowed ashes.

One child is missing,

Refugee Girls

— Survey

Half rainy,

half sunny,

I was passing through the middle of a day like that.

A refugee group volunteer held out a sticker:

"What would you need most if faced with a war or disaster like these children?"

I hesitated and put a sticker on the box in the survey that said 'Food and Water.'

The volunteer told me I was wrong.

He opened a worn-out file folder.

In Africa or some yet more distant country
I could saw a tent where refugee children were gathered.
He told me those young children were living in the worst environment.
Some children even give birth to children,

In places where children give birth,
more desperately needed than passports or food was tents.

Tents where nothing can be seen,
There is something

between the volunteer looking at the border and me.

Black children sitting packed together in a small tent
are casting looks with dry eyes in this direction.

Children starting to talk,
while I just look.

Children who keep talking to each other on a distant border,
a border of desperate light.

The tent over there is an exhibition hall of distant pain .

Half is silence,

half is weeping.

There is something between the black children and me.

Dapdong Church Is Disappearing.

I stroll along, leaving Dapdong Church on my right.
The distance that changes little by little as I walk on
keeps chasing me, while the moon is stabbed by the spire.

Half of the church is hanging in the air
like a doll in the hands of a ventriloquist.
An overturned world
where things that look like that
don't look like that.

The claw of a mechanical digger
constructing tourism resources
is digging into the shadow of the church.

A dark womb-like dome.
The bats that used to go flying into the bell tower
after making waves at sunset
know the elderly boy who used to be the bellringer.

In a picture the elderly boy showed me
once
the church was floundering after falling into the

water.

Was the god who would save that church hiding behind the moon?

What saved me from the puddle was a horse that smelled fishy.

I walk on in search of the other half of the church.

Like the moon, the streetlights chase me.

When we get to the church and opened the locked door,

there was the same church inside the church.

When I opened the door again, the church

continued to appear.

I was startled and hurried out of there.

As I walked, the walls of the church moved.
If I went to the left, the right side disappeared,
if I went to the right, the left side disappeared.

I quickly picked up my shadow
and climbed up a hill higher than the church.
I hung up my long shadow cast by the light of a street lamp
and lay down beside it.

Then, the great dome of the cathedral opened,
like a music box and in it
several mechanical diggers were dancing.

Transfer

Fish scales flash and disappear in the mist.

A returning train is coming.

Opening the door

the wind gets in with its shadow.

The shadow gradually crumbles and falls,

the floor becomes a puddle of water,

the tilting shadow,

the deep puddle,

the shadow falls, stumbles and stops

The wind gets on the train called oblivion again

and speeds through the night

Ghost Spider

Older sister,

am I dead?

Yes, you're dead.

Older sister,

I'm really dead, right?

Yes, and I had you cremated,

then I saw you turned into white powder in the grinding room.

This white jar is your new home now.

Older sister,

my stomach is aching fit to die!

You were always saying you were going to die, and now you're really dead,

so you're not going to die anymore.

Sister, the moonlight was so bright that day,

moonlight or waves, it was so beautiful I tossed and turned, you know.

Beautiful things are so intoxicating

that I drank on until dawn.

And then I suddenly disappeared.

Yet I was definitely wearing the shoes you bought me.

In an abandoned house,
borrowing a window,
a ghost spider is re-weaving the night.
Surging like waves
continuing on as if about to snap,
riding the waves of the wind.

Showing only a rear view,
stiff and hard.

A Nightmare and an Illusion

When I opened the red door, a cow was hanging on the wall.
A cow tattered like an unbuttoned garment with its head off.
The sticky blood was hardening in a basin.
After digging and pulling the inside of the wound out,
mouths calling the cow
mouths become the cow.

The red light hanging from the ceiling is shaking.
Stripping off the white fat, then separating the meat from the bones.

Becoming a cow together,
a constantly renewed illusion.
Pushing it into the hole that's been dug,
throwing it away again and again.

Like an experienced woman washing and dressing the dead,
half covering its face.
I saw a blue bruise
like a vine strangling and rising to the top of the head.
A woman who walked into her own yoke,
a woman who became a bruise.

As red light spreads from wall to wall,
the moment everything fell silent on the cutting board,
the woman who came running out of a dream,
at last,
could cut even the cow's shadow.
With bloodstained mouth,
with trembling hands
very
briefly

Shaking

A homeless woman with dishevelled hair is sleeping in front of a closed electric store.

As I walked around the neighborhood, in front of the Hyemyeong Dancheong Museum

I asked her, *Is this is a privately operated museum?*

The woman crouched there, holding out a blackened hand.

Give me a few coins?

I had some bank-notes, but she only asked for coins

and as I turned and walked away after giving her some coins, I felt regretful.

Should I go back?

But wouldn't that make her sadder still?

This kind of thing always makes me shake.

My younger brother asked me to send him some money again.

If I feel angry, I shake before my anger.

Why do you live like that? Aren't you going to get a job?

That's what I said to you when you were about to die.

The afternoon the death toll and unemployment figures passed across the electronic billboard.

I am stabbed by the words I spoke.

They turn into a swamp and I sink down.

All grief grows putting out roots into the air.
All abandoned roads are
like you,
my roots grow doing handstands in the air.

Shaking
just enough not to be shaking,
I live by that shaking.

Fog

Don't go into the reed bed, dear.

If the white heads of the reeds blow about, they'll poke you in the eye.

(Better not to be seen.)

If you go into the reed bed, I'll not be able to find you.

(Don't look for me! I'll cut off and throw away the hair behind your ears and your heels.)

Chimney Sweeper and Crow.

When my mother died I was very young,
And my father sold me while yet my tongue
Could scarcely cry " 'weep! 'weep! 'weep! 'weep!"
So your chimneys I sweep & in soot I sleep.
— W. Blake, from "*The Chimney Sweeper.*"

When I entered the chimney,
a black crow followed me in.
He jumped on my face and laughed at me.

Hey, what's wrong with your face?
It's full of gloomy clouds.

The crow called: Caw, caw.
After going through my empty wallet
it went into my old school bag.

Boy! What's this?
the matches are all soaked,
and what's up with the cloud doll?

I hate sweeping chimneys.
I feel as if I will become ashes in soot.
I saw the face of my dead brother in a dream.
He was trapped in a black box

with chimney sweeping boys younger than me.*

The end and the far end of the dark cliff,

chimneys birds enter and burn to death.

Boy! Is the bird dead?

Come on, quick, remove the ashes with your brush!

I also want to go to school

with a chimney butterfly.

**A variation on the poem by William Blake quoted above.*

Fish Star(Turned into Black Rain)

The stars are
shining cold in the distance,
watching to see who's crying.
The stars are
twinkling,
twinkling then crying together.
Crying, they forget that morning in coming.

They sink together into the cold sea.
Before the red sun rises,
they sink down deep
and become fish stars
that can't be rescued together.

The children who have become fish enter their
eyes
and cry together.
Torn fins
rub their wounds in water
and become the wounds of water.

Turned into black rain,
they are buried together at sea.

Gaps

Nights when I cannot love
the gap between one old tree and another old tree,
between one raindrop and other raindrops.

In the gap between one cloud and other clouds
the moon's shadow feels tired and lies down on
the road

Puddles and corners
forehead and ankles
shadows and ashes
not knowing one another

erasing everything and going.

Lightning strikes the ant's eye in passing.

The gap

where time lives

instead of us.

POET'S NOTES

My first collection of poems, "*We Decided to Get a Bit Darker*," tells the story of people living in the dark alleys of Incheon. For me, Incheon has always been a place of love and hate, hard to bear, that I longed to cast off. But that unbearable quality led me to become a poet.

In this collection of poems, only the place has changed, but it contains the stories of girls and boys living in dark alleys around the world. Their voices kept overflowing inside me, and I had no choice but to write them down.

poor seeds submerged in water,
screams slipping over cliffs,

I could not help it.

Could only write.

POET'S ESSAY

My Growing Boxes

1.

One day, I was walking around the open port area where I live. I was walking in the midst of sunlight. There was a clap of thunder and suddenly it began to rain. The sun went in, then came back out in the rain, sparkling as it grew wet on the ground. One day in a street in the middle of the day when the sun was slowly dying, a volunteer from a refugee organization approached me and asked me to answer a survey. "What do you need the most when you are faced with war or disaster like these children?" I hesitated and said it was food and water, then the volunteer showed me a picture and said that what the refugee girls most needed was not food or water, but a tent. She said that even children gave birth to children there. From that day on, the black eyes of the black children continued to follow me.

Half is silence,
half is weeping.
There is something between the black children and me. (Excerpt from "Rufugee girls—Survey")

For me, poetry is about finding that 'something'. Between corners and puddles, between laughing and crying, between barbarism and misery, that "something" comes to me and shakes me to wake me up. Tears, yet unnamed, cross my threshold and soak the dreams of my sleep.

The indescribable 'something', like sunlight that glitters in the rain and disappears, is so soft that I can touch it, then it becomes transparent and finally disappears. The questions that I raise while creaking with the world one day become poetry, and one day they fail to become poetry and fall over the cliff.

2.

This world is like a huge box, a box you build and break apartevery day. People live in boxes they make for themselves. The shape of each box is different, depending on each person's inner valley. My box changes every day. Yesterday's was different and tomorrow's will be different. Today, I am locked in a six-sided box. If I push on the walls one by one, fish-stars, tundra carnivores, macaw parrots, anthills, and tents pop out. In the corner of the wall, there is a bucket of anonymous tears that flow down like from a leaking faucet.

The inside of the box is getting bigger and bigger, so even a musk ox can easily fit in. One day, Dapdong Church came in. The dome of the cathedral opens and a crane dances like in a music box inside it. My box was getting bigger and bigger to fit the church. Another day, lightning struck the box, and tens of thousands of ants entered my head and buzzed. Inside the box, they were either lumped together or broken into small pieces like dust. Tears that had not yet been named were overflowing from a bucket.

Words with many leaves like trees.
Words with nothing on them like dead trees

The words that keep growing in my box and the questions that swallow the clock sometimes go too far and then come back. I don't know what box will appear in front of me tomorrow, and I don't know what tears will fall into the bucket,

Now I need more boxes to hold the sentences.

COMMENTARY

This letter is also meant for you.

Song Jong-won (Literary critic)

Reading poet Lee Sul-ya's poems is no different from walking through the fields of the heart that the poet has cultivated. It is difficult to predict that you will experience a relaxed and leisurely space just because I described it as walking. The world's pain is planted here and there in the poet's field, and the boundaries of the field are always full of various trees and stones that are difficult to cultivate comfortably. If you look into the field of the heart that the poet has cultivated, Lee Sul-ya is a poet who believes that caring for the pain spread around the world is no different from caring for herself and she is a poet who constantly tries to ask how far I can be myself. The task of interrogating one's boundaries is not just at the level of the poet establishing her identify. It is also a matter of looking at how I can exist more correctly in this world. So, this poet's poem says, "You are me, too," and also sings, "I am myself only when I embrace my outside." My outside and you are absolute beings equal to me, but the political economy in reality creates yous who are discriminated against, oppressed, and exploited. When Lee Sul-ya's poem says, "You are also me," that you is an acronym for me.

What I see is based on the life I live. Saying this may be a way of asking how narrow my way of seeing is. In "Refugee Girls — Survey," Lee Sul-a asks this question painfully. What do children need in situations such as refugees in war or disaster? Perhaps it is easy for anyone to regard food and water as most essential to survival, like the poet. However, what children most desperately need is tents. A life in desperate need of shade to shelter from the sunlight, a painful life in which a young life, one still too early to have a child, is in a position to give birth, and is not provided with the shelter necessary for a safe birth of the mother and child in the process of childbirth is a reality that is everywhere in this world. The poet sees a tent in this situation. A life that my gaze cannot reach or a place that I cannot imagine from my life. In order to reach there beyond the tent, the poet exits outside herself and looks for a place to see from. Therefore, in this poet's poems, attention is paid to the hardships of people beyond borders, and attention is also paid to persons who have suffered beyond time.

But why does the poet try to look outside of her life, worry about what she sees, and want to take care of it? Lee Sul-ya's poems makes us think about this problem. Moral justification can also be said to be an answer. Perhaps it is because the poet senses acutely that we are not living alone, but that we live together. A poet is a person who delicately senses the fact that he or she exchanges countless influences in relationship. I influence the world beyond my intentions, and the world also bestows countless powers on me. This relationship is not always easy. For example, the poem "Kindness" in this collection of poems illustrates this well. The poet knows that no matter what kindness you act with, the act does not guarantee good results as intended. That's why even more my actions are done looking out of me, and my thoughts must also accompany me. Of course, the actions and thoughts of poets can also be acts and thoughts with kindness. This means that the results may not always lead to fresh and good results. However, just because it is impossible to predict the results does not overshadow the value of current straight thoughts and actions. However, it is also true that such answers alone are not enough.

Lee Sul-ya is also a poet who is fascinated by the joy and secrecy of life in a life of solidarity and caring for each other. The opposite to saying that we may be indifferent to others or hurtful to others is to say that we are beings who can 'greet anyone' as the poet says in one poem. While greeting each other and holding hands and giving each other a look of comfort, we are freed from our respective prisons. In the poems of Lee Sul-ya, the sense of liberation at such moments is depicted as a white snowflake. Although it is an image that is extremely instantaneous and easily extinguished, the poet's language builds a snowman and waits through it. Therefore, the poet Lee Sul-ya is also a person who endures and waits. The world we live in is not a smoothly connected world, but a world that is somewhat out of joint. The dream wanted fails by the expectations of the person wanting every time, while understanding or communication are not done on time every time, but belatedly. Like a dislocated bone, the dislocated world brings us pain. However, the poet does not interpret dislocation as a tragedy and conclusion. The dislocated world for Lee Sul-ya is a condition in which new creation can occur. So, the poet launches poems that may be received late or whose recipients may be unclear, like letters. And a new time opens from the poems launched into the world. The poet will dream. That someone may interpret the world anew with her poems and may someone live the world differently with her poems. That's how a new time opens up. In addition, it should be pointed out that one person's place is everyones place. If it is not a place for everyone, but for someone specific and causing discrimination, the poet will think that the place is meaningless and unrelated to the new time.

WHAT THEY SAY ABOUT LEE SUL-YA

"*We Decided to Get Darker*" uses the sorrows, hardships, and tragedies of popular life, which were bound to be the fundamental emotions of Realism in the 70s and 80s, so it embraces the appearance of a defector trying to flee far away from them by boldly introducing motifs surrounded by fairy tales.

Lee Chan, "Symphonic Rhythm of Bodies",
Lyric Poetry Quarterly, 2017.

Poems that have been polished for a long time may lose transparency and become murky, but these are as hard and clear as pebbles polished in water as if they had been through a long refining process. Lee Sul-ya's poems have a full face of reality, as if she wanted to escape from the gloomy and heavy emotions of the end of the century, but if language play and autistic poetry writing were helpless and irresponsible under a realistic load, Lee Solyas poetry confronts reality directly. If her poems often seem to lose their way, it is because she seems to be trapped in this reality without an exit and unable to escape from. Paradoxically, I think that the poets quality lies precisely at this point. It is an attitude that refused to avoid the reality in front of it even if it reaches a point where it is impossible to get out of it by itself. This allows her to find her own exit at the very nadir without turning her eyes toward a bypass exit. Her poetic performance tells us that this method is not reckless.

Kim Sa-in and Baek Musan, "The 1st Gosan Literature Awards New Writers Award" Judges Report, 2017.

Lee Sul-ya is in the limelight of realism in that she actively engages in the fight against the still persistent coercive social structures and the reality of human alienation. At the same time, she is supporting modernism in that she tries to heal the wounded inner side by scolding it in her own language. Because of this characteristic, I would like to consider Lee Sul-ya as a natural "convergent realist" and a mature poet.

Jung Woo-young, "A Mariner in the Age that decided to grow darker", *Literatures*, 2017.

K-POET
Cave Boys

Written by Lee Sul-ya
Translated by Brother Anthony of Taizé
Published by ASIA Publishers
Address 445, Hoedong-gil, Paju-si, Gyeonggi-do, Korea
Tel (8231).955.7958
Fax (8231).955.7956
Email bookasia@hanmail.net
Homepage Address www.bookasia.org

ISBN 979-11-5662-317-5 (set) | 979-11-5662-567-4 (04810)
First published in Korea by ASIA Publishers 2021

This book is published with the support of the Literature Translation Institute of Korea (LTI Korea).

can meet the real Korea!

Korean Literature

22 keywords to understand Korean literature

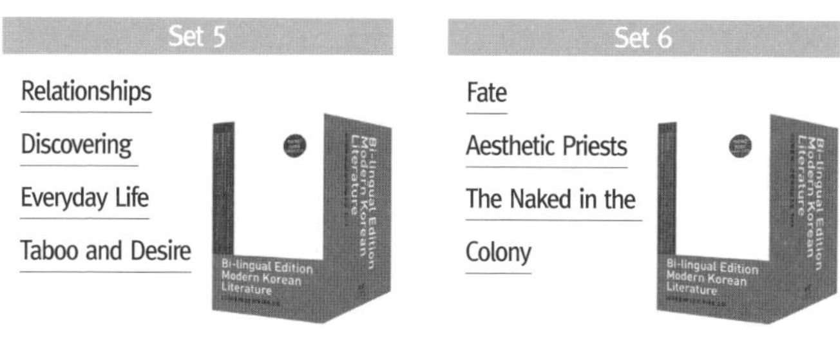

Set 7

Colonial Intellectuals Turned "Idiots"

Traditional Korea's Lost Faces

Before and After Liberation

Korea After the Korean War

korean literature"on Amazon!

K-픽션 한국 젊은 소설

최근에 발표된 단편소설 중 가장 우수하고 흥미로운 작품을 엄선하여 출간하는 〈K-픽션〉은 한국문학의 생생한 현장을 국내외 독자들과 실시간으로 공유하고자 기획되었습니다. 원작의 재미와 품격을 최대한 살린 〈K-픽션〉 시리즈는 매 계절마다 새로운 작품을 선보입니다.

001 버핏과의 저녁 식사-**박민규** Dinner with Buffett-**Park Min-gyu**

002 아르판-**박형서** Arpan-**Park hyoung su**

003 애드벌룬-**손보미** Hot Air Balloon-**Son Bo-mi**

004 나의 클린트 이스트우드-**오한기** My Clint Eastwood-**Oh Han-ki**

005 이베리아의 전갈-**최민우** Dishonored-**Choi Min-woo**

006 양의 미래-**황정은** Kong's Garden-**Hwang Jung-eun**

007 대니-**윤이형** Danny-**Yun I-hyeong**

008 퇴근-**천명관** Homecoming-**Cheon Myeong-kwan**

009 옥화-**금희** Ok-hwa-**Geum Hee**

010 시차-**백수린** Time Difference-**Baik Sou linne**

011 올드 맨 리버-**이장욱** Old Man River-**Lee Jang-wook**

012 권순찬과 착한 사람들-**이기호** Kwon Sun-chan and Nice People-**Lee Ki-ho**

013 알바생 자르기-**장강명** Fired-**Chang Kangmyoung**

014 어디로 가고 싶으신가요-**김애란** Where Would You Like To Go?-**Kim Ae-ran**

015 세상에서 가장 비싼 소설-**김민정** The World's Most Expensive Novel-**Kim Min-jung**

016 체스의 모든 것-**김금희** Everything About Chess-**Kim Keum-hee**

017 할로윈-**정한아** Halloween-**Chung Han-ah**

018 그 여름-**최은영** The Summer-**Choi Eunyoung**

019 어느 피씨주의자의 종생기-**구병모** The Story of P.C.-**Gu Byeong-mo**

020 모르는 영역-**권여선** An Unknown Realm-**Kwon Yeo-sun**

021 4월의 눈-**손원평** April Snow-**Sohn Won-pyung**

022 서우-**강화길** Seo-u-**Kang Hwa-gil**

023 가출-**조남주** Run Away-**Cho Nam-joo**

024 연애의 감정학-**백영옥** How to Break Up Like a Winner-**Baek Young-ok**

025 창모-**우다영** Chang-mo-**Woo Da-young**

026 검은 방-**정지아** The Black Room-**Jeong Ji-a**